THEY DIED TOO YOUNG

JOHN CANDY

Phelan Powell

CHELSEA HOUSE PUBLISHERS

Philadelphia

Printed and bound in Malaysia.
First Printing
1 3 5 7 9 8 6 4 2

Photographs courtesy of: Archive Photos, London Features
International Ltd. and Photofest.

Cover photo:
John Candy in the 1992 film *Once Upon a Crime*.
Courtesy Photofest

Library of Congress Cataloging-in-Publication Data
Powell, Phelan.
    John Candy / Phelan Powell.
        p. cm. - (They died too young)
    Filmography: p.
    Includes bibliographical references and index.
    Summary: Chronicles the life of actor and comedian John Candy, as
well as his death in 1994.
    ISBN 0-7910-5226-5
        1. Candy, John-Juvenile literature.   2. Comedians-Canada-
Biography-Juvenile literature.   3. Motion picture actors and
actresses-Canada-Biography-Juvenile literature.   [1. Comedians.
2. Actors and actresses.]   I. Title.   II. Series.
    PN2308.C36P68   1999
    791.43'028'092-dc21
    [B]   99-12312
                                                         CIP

9|05
Jollott
$19.95

Publishing Coordinator Jim McAvoy
Contributing Editors Bruce Durost Fish, Becky Durost Fish
Digital Design, Book Production Robert Gerson

ABOUT THE AUTHOR

Phelan Powell has worked as a daily correspondent for the
Michigan City News-Dispatch. Earlier, Phelan wrote feature articles
and created a cartoon strip for college newspapers. The author of
Chelsea House books on Tom Cruise and John LeClair, Phelan is
currently working on other books for Chelsea House Publishers.

CONTENTS

John Candy with costar Steve Martin in the 1987 film
Planes, Trains and Automobiles

A NEED TO BELONG

The streets of New York City teemed with frantic holiday travelers anxious to flee the confines of their tedious office day. Neal Page, a well-dressed, over-stressed advertising executive, scanned the stream of traffic, looking for a cab to take to the airport.

After several missed attempts, he ran for one seemingly empty taxi, only to find it occupied by a huge man with a pair of warm, innocent eyes which perched angelically above a brown caterpillar mustache accenting a smiling set of lips.

Thus began the 1987 film comedy, *Planes, Trains and Automobiles*, which finally made John Candy a Hollywood success after years of acting.

As the movie unfolded, Candy, who played Del Griffith, had a sunbeam face, which lit up the brooding, dark atmosphere of the airport terminal waiting area filled with grumpy people, who, like Neal Page, just wanted to get home to their families for Thanksgiving.

As Neal, played by Steve Martin, and Del were thrown together, Del consistently showed an ability to rise to any occasion and make the best of things, much to Neal's frustration. Once on the airplane, the two found themselves seated next to each other, but Del's bulk uncomfortably spilled out of his own seat and into Neal's precious space.

Neal Page had no use for this seemingly good-natured man who had the unconscious nerve to remove his shoes as he sprawled on the seat next to him.

Everything was a problem for the single-minded Neal, but Del Griffith was always the person trying to make others feel comfortable. Such was the real John Candy, who was known to go into a restaurant kitchen and make the kitchen workers feel loved and appreciated. He would not only help them cook, but he'd also invite them to his house afterward.

The priceless scene Candy and Martin enacted in the motel room in Wichita, Kansas, where the two were stranded, will stand forever in viewers' minds. Del popped beers which exploded onto the single bed the two had to share. He cracked his knuckles, cracked his neck, and worked on eliminating phlegm, which in a less brilliantly acted scene would have had the audience suffering severe bouts of nausea. Instead, Neal Page's scathing critique of Del Griffith's habits resulted in an explanation of the kindly salesman's faults.

"I am the real article," he told Page. And in life Candy was always the real article, often to his detriment, as he fell for one bad business deal after another. Passionately and truly, he sought approval and love from those who were closest to him.

The horror of Neal Page's Thanksgiving journey next found him on a bus filled with what could best be called the common man. Neal gamely tried to get those he obviously thought were beneath him to join in with his singing of an old show tune. Needless to say, it did not fly. Only when Del Griffith let loose with a rousing rendition of the *Flintstones* theme song did the captive audience come alive.

This scene showed how much of an "everyman" John Candy was to his loyal audiences. Viewers could always identify with his pain, embarrassment, heartaches, and good naturedness.

Neal Page, mystified by this strange and often painful creature, claimed Del Griffith was a charmed man.

They Died Too Young

"No," said Del, frankly, "I just go with the flow."

That is what John Candy did with his life. And his flow was a fast-moving river that he never hesitated to jump into.

Another heart-stopping moment in *Planes, Trains and Automobiles* was when Del was driving Neal in a wreck of a car going the wrong way down a seriously fast highway. Del did not realize he was feeling so warm because a lit cigarette he had inadvertently flicked into the back seat was starting a fire. He attempted to remove his heavy jacket and ended up catching both his sleeves on car parts which left him unable to drive the car with his hands.

It was at the end of his life that John Candy actually did lose control of parts of his life, and perhaps that resulted in his much too early demise.

In *Planes, Trains and Automobiles,* Del Griffith reveals to his unwilling friend Neal Page that when he leaves this world "all that I have to prove that I was here are some shower rings."

That may have been the fictional Del Griffith's belief, but years after John Candy's death, his fans still enjoy his movies, no matter what the critics have said.

*John Candy portrayed producer, entrepreneur, wheeler-dealer
Johnny LaRue on the SCTV show*

FINDING A PLACE

On October 31, 1950, a day when candy was given out freely in celebration of Halloween, Evangeline Candy gave birth to her second son, John Franklin Candy. His father, Sidney, and older brother by two years, Jim, welcomed the new addition to their family and their home on a quiet street in King City just north of Toronto. His father was a World War II veteran who saw action in Germany and North Africa. Although details of that combat experience weren't discussed, the family was aware that those experiences overseas had been traumatic.

In later years, John was asked about his father during an interview with *Parade Magazine.*

"He had a lot of psychological scars," Candy said of his father. "He'd wake up in sweats. He bounced from job to job. He finally got his own used-car lot, Champion Motors."

Nonetheless, John's life was pretty normal for the first five years, until the unthinkable happened. Death struck mercilessly, felling Sidney with a heart attack. At the age of 35, the man John knew and loved as Dad was taken from him. And for the young family, life would never be the same.

John's memory of his first funeral remained with him throughout his life.

"I didn't know why he died," he remembered. "I never understood it. Later, when I had kids, I realized how much I missed him and needed him. I didn't have a role model."

The family left King City shortly after the tragedy and moved to the Toronto suburb of East York. Rather than remain alone, Evangeline and the boys shared a house with her sister and her parents. John attended Holy Cross Catholic School where he was an average student but well-liked for his pleasing personality and helpful nature. Like many young boys in Catholic school, he participated in Mass as an altar boy.

When he was old enough, he helped the family out financially by working at a department store in downtown Toronto. His mother and aunt also worked there.

Television came of age during John's childhood, and like many children, he spent hours absorbed in the fantasy the new medium provided. Movies were another big entertainment outlet for him. It cost as little as a quarter to see a feature at the time, and John joined the hundreds of kids who would fill the theaters several times a week to watch the antics of the stars. Although few could tell at the time, the loss of his father made him feel sad and depressed, and he realized early on that acting could help him deal with those feelings.

"I think I may have become an actor to hide from myself," John admitted in later years. "You can escape into a character. You can get lost and take up another life."

John went to Neil McNeil High, a Catholic high school near the shore of Lake Ontario. He involved himself in school life, playing clarinet in the band and serving on the student council. He was never comfortable with his large size, but he found a place where his bulk was a positive thing—the football field. As an offensive tackle, Candy allowed few of his opponents to get by him. He loved the game and would remain an avid fan his entire life, but his playing days were cut short when he suffered a knee injury.

John needed a class to fill his schedule and ended up, quite by accident, in a drama class. It was not long before a few of

They Died Too Young

the small parts he was given turned into comedic opportunities. Candy, who was always eager to please, enjoyed the appreciative laughter of the audiences as they watched him mug his way through his roles. The applause was all the more valuable to him since he felt like a bit of an outcast socially. John knew and was liked by many of the kids at school, but girls were not usually interested in him romantically. Because of his grades, he was taking a diploma course at McNeil instead of enrolling in classes which would prepare him for university, which is how Canadians usually refer to college.

By the time Candy neared graduation from McNeil, the Vietnam conflict had been dragging on for years. Toronto had become a haven for Americans who had fled over the border to avoid the draft. John decided he wanted to be a U.S. Marine and headed to Buffalo, New York, to enlist. His plan was short-lived, however, because his bad knee proved problem enough for the Marines to reject his application.

Candy finished high school and, with little enthusiasm, started classes at Centennial College in Scarborough, an area in the eastern section of Toronto. As many youths his age, John had no idea what he wanted to do with his life at this point. He took journalism but had little interest in the courses or even in attending them.

"I was a confused young man," said John in later years. "I didn't know what I wanted to be. Football was out because I'd hurt my knee. I had a series of odd jobs—selling sporting goods, mixing paint—you name it. One of my jobs was working with an ice show. I drove a small portable rink around. I made the ice. It was one of my first tastes of show business."

It was not long before John switched his courses, giving up journalism and taking on more theater courses. He was slowly defining himself as an actor. John was still working as a department store clerk and attending classes when he got his first paying job as an actor. A talent agent he knew, Catherine McCartney, realized John was desperate for a break into show business and eventually approached him with a part in a commercial, playing, of all things, a football player.

That commercial was followed soon after by another, and Candy knew by then that acting was the only thing he wanted to do. McCartney found John likable, and she did whatever she could to get auditions for him.

"John had the ability to make people feel special even if he had only known them a short time. Once he became your friend, he was always there for you, to listen and provide a shoulder to cry on," McCartney stated.

By the end of 1971, John was performing in his first professional play, an original effort called *Creeps*.

It was a small part, and during the play's run, John made $40 a week. But it made him a professional actor, and finally having a direction for his life made all the difference in the world. Things were looking up, even in the romantic department.

John had met a student at the Ontario College of Art, by the name of Rosemary Hobor, and he and she would often go out with friends after his performances at the Tarragon Theatre. To help with expenses, John took a job with a paper company which required him to sell their items door-to-door.

"I was terrible at it," John recalled. "Out of forty salesmen, I was number forty. I was having so much fun doing theater my heart just wasn't in flogging napkins."

That fact was not hidden from his boss at the paper company. Within a short time, John was fired. But John did not take the action personally, for he knew the job had just been a short detour on his way to making a living as an actor. He vowed to take only acting jobs, no matter how little they paid.

More regular theater work came John's way in early 1972 when the Caravan Theatre hired him to perform for their children's touring group. The troupe did indoor theater performances, as well as shows in parks throughout the city. Very often, John found himself cast as an inanimate object, but his stage presence was such that no matter what the role, his performances stood out.

In 1972 John Candy and Dan Aykroyd met. Aykroyd considered himself a comic more than an actor and in 1972 ran, with a friend, a small after-hours club in downtown Toronto.

After a spring and summer with the Caravan Theatre touring group, Candy signed on with another children's theater group called the Jolly Jesters. The troupe specialized in school performances. John was an important member of the small group of actors—and not just because he was a promising acting talent. He was also in charge of driving the group's van with all the necessary stage equipment to and from performances. As stage manager he made $65 a week. Schools usually paid the Jolly Jesters $100 to perform their versions of classic literary pieces such as *Treasure Island*.

At the end of 1972, John was once again performing at the Tarragon Theatre. This time he had a part in an adult fairy tale called *The Stag King*. He had spent the year paying his dues as a struggling actor in small, low-paying performances, but he was loving the life. And 1973 would prove to be a year brimming with new opportunities.

John Candy with many of the original members of Second City *and the* SCTV Network *including, Eugene Levy (back row, left), Rick Moranis (back row, right), Joe Flaherty (front row, center), and Andrea Martin (front row, right)*

SECOND CITY

Centuries ago traveling troupes of actors would go from town to town and perform loosely structured skits, using audience participation to spice up each performance.

This idea gave birth to acting groups in Chicago during the 1950s, and at the end of that decade they became the company known as Second City. The name Second City came from an article someone had written calling Chicago the "Second City" compared to New York City.

Many of the most popular performers in America started out on the stage of Second City's comedy club in Chicago. By the early 1970s actors such as Alan Arkin and Valerie Harper and comedians Joan Rivers and David Steinberg had already graduated and moved on to bigger and better career opportunities.

One of the founders of Second City, Bernie Sahlins, came to Toronto in 1973 because he believed the city would be a good place to open another Second City comedy club. He liked Toronto's location in relation to the lively, entertainment-loving populations of New York, Chicago, Boston, and Washington. When Sahlins came to Toronto, he recruited the likes of Gilda Radner for the new group. Actor/comedian Brian Doyle Murray was working for Second City in Chicago at the time. Sahlins sent Murray to Toronto to help train the new recruits.

Sahlins liked what he saw in John Candy and sent him immediately to Chicago to train with the veterans. By 1973, John had learned a lot about life in Toronto, but he was very nervous about his move to the big city of Chicago.

"I'd never really been away from Toronto before, and I had all these weird images of Chicago. I guess it went back to my infatuation with *The Untouchables* on TV. Once I got there I realized [gangster] Al Capone and [FBI agent] Frank Nitti weren't around any more."

Comedian Bill Murray was in Chicago when John arrived, and to Candy's relief, Murray did his best to make his new friend very comfortable in the Windy City.

"He took me all over the city, showed me every landmark," John said appreciatively. "We'd have a hamburger at the original McDonald's, a pancake at the first International House of Pancakes. We went to every weird, seedy area imaginable. He'd always say 'This is my town and this can be your town too.' When we'd go to Wrigley Field he knew every Cubs player that had ever lived. In fact, I had my first case of sunstroke seeing a Cubs game."

John's first year in Chicago went quickly, but it was a year he thoroughly enjoyed. His girlfriend, Rosemary Hobor, had come down to join him, and John, known in Chicago as "Johnny Toronto," made many friends. But Bernie Sahlins wanted him to go back to Toronto at the end of 1973 and help breathe some life into the wobbly Second City organization on Lombard Street.

While John Candy was having a great time learning and partying in Chicago, Second City in Toronto began during the summer in a small theater on Adelaide Street and died there a scant five months later. The venture suffered from inadequate advertising, uncomfortable seating, and the lack of the one thing that always draws some people, no matter what the entertainment—a liquor license.

But there where those in Toronto who believed in the concept, such as Andrew Alexander, a man who lived to promote things. He was broke at the time he attempted to resurrect Second City, but that did not stop him. Alexander bought the rights to Second City from Bernie Sahlins for one dollar. He

They Died Too Young

then convinced enough investors that Second City could live again and ended up with enough money to turn an old beer hall on Lombard Street into a theater/restaurant.

The initial group that got things going again was comprised of John Candy, Joe Flaherty, Gilda Radner, Eugene Levy, and Rosemary Radcliffe. Second City was an American invention, and at first the young actors found themselves concentrating on satirical sketches of life in the U.S. But Toronto audiences wanted something of their own, and in a short time the Second City material was tailored to fit that need.

One particularly successful skit the group performed in the early days was called, "You're Going To Be All Right, You Creep, Leaving Home and All, Eh?" A lot of plays about dysfunctional families were being done in Canadian theater at that time, and the Second City parody of a family's angst became an immediate hit with audiences.

John Candy played the normal hockey-loving Canadian son whose brother was gay and whose sister was mentally challenged. The father was a heavy-handed tyrant, and the mother just tried to be the glue to hold the troubled family together.

The actors had a lot of fun in the early days, experimenting with new ideas and perfecting routines that worked like a charm.

Gilda Radner, who was to go on to achieve great fame and fortune before she died of ovarian cancer in 1989, once spoke about the early Second City troupe in Toronto.

"Something incredible would happen onstage. . . . Later, you'd be so excited about what happened, you couldn't sleep at night. You'd be trying to remember exactly what made it click so well and made it come together like a piece of art, with rising action and a climax and an end."

It was in this stimulating environment that John Candy grew out of his "new kid on the block" status and into a seasoned actor/comedian who never failed to engage the interest of audiences whenever they saw him. John lived for the applause and received $160 for a week's work with the group.

In 1974, he had a chance to expand his horizons by auditioning for a children's television show. Canadian boys and girls watched syndicated American TV shows on the Canadian Broadcasting Company (CBC) station. But station managers were looking to provide local programming for their young viewers.

A show called *Dr. Zonk and the Zunkins* was developed and scheduled to be shown two times a week after school. Each *Dr. Zonk* show was composed of a number of comedy sketches, so many of the Second City performers auditioned. John Candy's natural friendliness made him an easy pick for the cast. He gladly signed on and very happily agreed to the pay, which was $200 per day.

Also in 1974, John landed a small part in a Canadian movie, *It Seemed Like a Good Idea at the Time,* where his comedic talents were used in his role as a goofy detective.

But all the while, Candy was under the delicious pressure to improvise, improvise, improvise on the stage on Lombard Street. Second City in Chicago and Toronto had achieved such widespread fame that Bernie Sahlins and Andrew Alexander decided they would open a Second City club in California in 1975.

The site they chose was in a shopping mall in Pasadena, but instead of calling it Second City Pasadena, they named it Alterations While U Wait, which confused mall-goers into thinking it was a tailor's shop. John Candy was sent out to the new venture several times during that year.

John was excited about going to California, for never far from his mind was the possibility that his biggest break yet might come while he was in Hollywood. It was not to be, though he did get a bit part in a goofy movie called *Tunnelvision*. Not only did the role not propel John to stardom, it hardly paid him at all. The movie was made on a very small budget. John was not alone in the venture, however, for his friend Bill Murray had signed onto the project. Another star of the future, Chevy Chase, also ended up on the set with Candy and Murray.

After a few months, the Pasadena venture folded, and John went back to Second City in Toronto again.

They Died Too Young

NEW BEGINNINGS

John Candy took a short detour on the comedy highway in 1976 when he signed on to do a serious role in a movie called *The Clown Murders.* The movie was based on a true story of a woman in Ontario who had been kidnapped from a Halloween party and held for ransom in 1969. John played one of the hapless gang members responsible for the kidnapping.

Said writer/director Martyn Burke of Candy's work: "John was a puppy dog on the set. He was an overgrown kid, and everyone loved him. He seemed very hungry for approval. Some actors go out of their way to gain the approval of the producer or the director in a professional way, but John seemed to want it on a personal level as well."

Like many of John's career efforts, *The Clown Murders* was neither a commercial nor artistic success, but it showed he could do more than comedy.

Following the movie stint, John became a popular presence on Canadian TV during 1976. He worked on several shows: *Coming Up Rosie, 90 Minutes Live,* and *The David Steinberg Show.* In the fall of that year, John signed on to a show which was to become a rival of the popular American weekly comedy *Saturday Night Live.*

Named *SCTV,* the Canadian offering poked fun at the least desirable aspects of television production and viewing. Many of the actors who perfected their craft on the Toronto Second

City stage had moved on to the bright lights and bigger money of *Saturday Night Live*. Andrew Alexander and Bernard Sahlins wanted to create a comedy vehicle that would be so lucrative that its comedians would not feel it was just a stepping-stone to better markets elsewhere.

SCTV began with six performers who were all veterans of Second City in Toronto: Dave Thomas, Catherine O'Hara, Andrea Martin, Eugene Levy, Joe Flaherty, and John Candy all signed on to do the TV show. Thirteen half-hour productions were shot in the Global Network studios on a very low budget, initially just $35,000 a show.

Having worked on the small stages of local Toronto clubs, John Candy was used to low production budgets and lower salaries, and he did not hold much hope that *SCTV* would be any different.

"Our producers found the cheapest studio and made the cheapest deal possible," John remembered. "Being the simpletons that we were at the time, we accepted their offer."

The cast did not rely on the skits which had worked in the old Second City format. They concentrated on freewheeling spoofs which satirized the world of television, in front of and behind the camera. All the actors participated in the making and writing of each episode. Writing was not John Candy's strength. He preferred acting out what others had put together.

"John Candy took the limelight, as did Andrea Martin, because his vulnerability was right out there, and no matter what character he was playing, he was always John Candy. The audience knew who he was and loved him and responded to that vulnerability," said Sahlins.

In a short time, John Candy fans came to look forward to the regular characters he created for *SCTV,* whose fictional town of Melonville housed such people as Mayor Tommy Shanks, Dr. Tongue, and an old standby John had used in his Second City sketches, the ill-mannered, bad-tempered Johnny LaRue.

They Died Too Young

"He had an instinct that everyone in the group trusted. He wasn't the most prolific writer, and there were others who brought more brain power and analysis to the material," said George Bloomfield, who was hired as the director of *SCTV* during its second year on television. "His special talent was for what he could do in lifting something off the page. He could take something that didn't seem that funny when you read it and turn it into something hilarious. He was the most predictably unpredictable member of the cast."

"John would always extend a sketch beyond what you anticipated, and I got into the habit of telling the cameramen not to stop when I called 'cut' because so often John would do something brilliant after he thought the scene was over. My credo was that if I laughed it was funny, and if I didn't laugh it wasn't funny. Sometimes John made me laugh so hard I would go home in pain. Once I fell off the chair backward because of what he did when he was playing the Incredible Hulk."

The fact that John did very little of the writing caused a bit of an upset for him during his *SCTV* days when he found out that some of the other performers were making more money that he was. When he discovered the difference in paychecks, he was told that those who wrote made more because of their contribution to the skits. It was a sore point for Candy for a long while, but his unhappiness never showed up in the productions.

SCTV was eventually compared with *Saturday Night Live,* which was performed before a New York City audience. Many who watched even thought *SCTV* was the better show of the two because of its intellectual approach to satire. George Bloomfield saw John Candy blossom during his tenure as director of the Canadian show.

"He wanted to improve," Bloomfield remembered. "Because I had come from the world of drama and his focus was comedy, he welcomed the coming together. His approach to comedy was character. I could see he was very inventive. That came out of something in his nature. On a personal level, John's generosity was striking. When he threw a party it was not just hot dogs. There would be some people from work there, and then there would be a whole pile of other people who had nothing to do with show business."

Bloomfield appreciated John's relationship with his sweetheart, Rosemary Hobor.

"He was drawn to real people rather than the showbiz crowd. That's where he would get his ideas and characters —people walking through malls. Rose was an earth mother. She was a potter, and he was proud of the work she did. For him it was a plus that she had nothing to do with the entertainment business."

The Global Television Network cancelled *SCTV* after its third year, but it mattered little to John. He was a compulsive workaholic and already had new projects in the works.

In 1978, he got a part in a Canadian movie called *The Silent Partner*, playing an average, serious bank clerk and got to rub shoulders with a Hollywood star, Christopher Plummer.

Lost and Found, John's next film, was an American movie which was filmed mainly in Canada. His was a comedic role in which he performed with such actors as George Segal and Glenda Jackson. His part was small but challenging—he played a 55-year-old French used-car salesman while he was still in his twenties.

Candy was getting used to the glamour of working with top Hollywood stars, and he had the opportunity to work with famous Hollywood director Steven Spielberg for his next film.

Spielberg was the name on every moviegoer's lips after his smash box-office hits *Jaws* and *Close Encounters of the Third Kind*. For his next film, Spielberg had chosen to direct a film which spoofed the nervous commotion in the city of Los Angeles just after the bombing of Pearl Harbor. It was to be called *1941*. When Spielberg approached John to take a part in the movie, John Candy thought the director was pulling his leg. He wasn't, and Candy jumped at the chance.

John acted alongside the likes of Dan Aykroyd and John Belushi, who had already made a name for themselves in the field of comedy. Unfortunately, *1941* was to be one of the few box-office bombs of Spielberg's career. But John believed every experience has its usefulness, and he knew that the six months he had put into acting in the film had been a time for making connections for the future.

Spielberg's movie had not been the highlight of 1979 for John, but even if it had been a roaring success it could not have measured up to one other event which occurred in April of that year. That was the day John took Rosemary, known as "Rosie," to be his wife.

With Dan Aykroyd and John Belushi in
Steven Spielberg's film **1941**

Undaunted by the failure of *1941*, John searched the horizon for his next project. A fellow Canadian export who worked out of Hollywood in 1979 remembered the way John Candy was then.

"John Candy was like a man on a train that was clearly going somewhere," Garry Blye recalled. "At the end of every project, he always had the sense that there was something better just around the corner, and he was in a rush to get to it. He wouldn't spend more than a week without work of some kind."

He felt the afterglow of being in a hit movie when he took a role in *The Blues Brothers,* which was released in 1980. The story, which got so-so reviews, was about two inept musicians played by Dan Aykroyd and John Belushi, who spend most of their screen time running from lawmen, one of whom was parole officer John Candy. Most of John's performance was edited from the final film, but even his minor role helped him make a bigger name for himself in Hollywood.

The box-office success of *The Blues Brothers* was eclipsed in 1980 by the birth of John and Rosemary's first child, a girl named Jennifer. By the summer of that year, John was starring in a Canadian television show called *Big City Comedy,* and on one of the shows he introduced his audience to his new pride and joy.

After 13 weeks, the show, which showcased some brilliant comedic sketches on John's part, was canceled, and John was on the prowl again for more work. It was to come in the form of a military comedy called *Stripes.*

John played an overweight Army recruit named Dewey Oxberger, nicknamed Ox. Ivan Reitman was another Canadian who had fled the north to seek his fortune under the bright lights of Hollywood. By the time he produced *Stripes* he had already become fabulously wealthy from the huge success of his film *Animal House.*

In *Stripes,* John worked with Bill Murray and Harold Ramis. His role was smaller than theirs, but he made it memorable. Initially John had his doubts that he would make a good impression in the role.

"The original character didn't look like much," John said in an interview with *Toronto Star* reporter Ron Base. "But Ivan said we could change it and I could do some writing. Everything fell together and we realized it could be a lot of fun."

John had always been a big man, and his wide girth made him a huge cuddly bear in the eyes of his fans. But in his eyes, his size was a touchy subject and a source of insecurity. In one scene in *Stripes,* Candy was supposed to wallow in mud with six women in a mud-wrestling match. He hated the thought of filming what he thought would make him look ridiculous.

His friend George Bloomfield remembered receiving a call from Candy about the scene.

"He was very worried about the character he was playing, and questioned what he was doing," Bloomfield recalled. "He wondered whether he was doing the right thing by participating in the mud-wrestling scene. He was afraid it might make him come across as a pig in the mud. He felt degraded."

John referred to the incident in an interview: "I was fighting right up to the end to get out of it. It was so painful, and we spent three days doing it. If you're going to mud-wrestle with six women, you want to do it in private. It's somewhat inhibiting when there are three hundred people watching," he said.

As it turned out, there was at least one review of that scene in the movie which Candy found degrading. The reviewer referred to Candy as an "elephant." In a *People* magazine interview, Candy made no bones about how he felt about the reviewer.

"Jerks like that are obvious," he said. "I'm sensitive about my weight. I'm the one who has to look in the mirror, and after a while it begins to eat at you."

In 1981, *SCTV* was being wooed by NBC in the United States, and John Candy was asked to return to the set. It was filmed in Edmonton, Canada, and its 1981 budget was a monstrous $475,000 an episode, a far cry from the mere $35,000 an episode when John had worked for it before. Another big change was that *SCTV* was to be a 90-minute show, an hour longer than the old one.

Due to the large budget, the actors found they had a lot more flexibility in the creation of their characters, particularly in the area of makeup.

"The sophistication of the make-up team opened doors for the performers and allowed them to do whatever they wanted to do," said associate producer Jason Shubb. "People like Beverley Schectman and Judy Cooper Sealy were geniuses in their field. The process was very labor intensive. One of the performers might have to spend four hours a day in the make-up chair, and it was exhausting. But everyone on the show was young and creative, and willing to work extremely hard. We all felt we were breaking new ground."

One of John Candy's most popular characters on the show turned out to be Yosh Schmenge, one of the two Schmenge Brothers. He and long-time friend and fellow actor Eugene Levy, who took the role of Stan Schmenge, played polka-playing immigrants from the make-believe land of Leutonia. Yosh played the clarinet and Stan played the accordion. Both were adorned with huge, distracting facial moles and slicked-back greasy looking hair. The characterizations were such a hit that when *SCTV* finally went off the air in 1983, after capturing U.S. television's highest award, an Emmy, the studio shot a final farewell to the duo with an hour-long special, *The Last Polka*.

Bad news came to John Candy in March 1982 with the untimely death of his friend and fellow-actor John Belushi. Belushi, like Candy, was supremely talented but overweight and known to overindulge when eating, drinking, and using drugs. John took Belushi's death hard and considered it a personal wake-up call to get himself into better shape. Besides being haunted by the specter of his father's early death due to heart problems, John also had to deal with the problem of drug abuse. John had often kiddingly referred to his days in Chicago with the Second City troupe as a time when he "learned how to stay up real late and spell d-r-u-g-s." But it took another two years before he seriously addressed his weight problem and went on a regimented diet.

John worked exclusively on *SCTV* until the summer of 1982, when he was given his first starring role in a Hollywood film. It was called *Going Berserk*.

John Candy and Eugene Levy as Yosh and Stan Schmenge in The Last Polka, *an HBO Comedy Playhouse special*

*John Candy with costar Tom Hanks in
Ron Howard's 1984 film,* Splash

CHANGING OPPORTUNITIES

Having a starring role in a film would have been a real boost to John's prolific career had the movie been a raving success at the box office. John was cast in a romantic role as a hefty limousine driver whose fiancée is the daughter of a U.S. congressman. Reviews pegged the film as being top-heavy with plot and lacking the energy to carry it out.

John did, as usual, manage to shine through the curtain of the film's fault. *New York Times* film critic Janet Masling, in an October 29, 1983 review, dubbed John "irrepressible," but immediately after its release, *Going Berserk* sank out of sight like a stone tossed into a pond.

In the end, John felt that, although it had been a less than successful film, making *Going Berserk* had its lessons from which he could learn.

In mid-1983, he had purchased a dream home in Canada just north of his birthplace, and when he finished *Going Berserk* he relaxed a bit there with his wife and daughter.

After that brief hiatus, workaholic John embarked on a much more pleasant film experience. Ron Howard was the director for the movie *Splash,* and John had a featured role acting with Tom Hanks and Daryl Hannah. Candy played a character much like his Johnny LaRue persona in *Second City* and *SCTV*: an amiable, devil-may-care party person who needs his bad habits to fuel an overwhelming desire to be liked.

Splash received rave reviews and was a big success at the

box office, but oddly enough, John shrugged off the glowing critiques.

"It wasn't Willy Loman (in *Death of a Salesman*) or *King Lear*," he told interviewer Martin Knelman for an article in *Toronto Life*. "People said 'Wow, you can really act.' Hell, I was just doing what I've been doing for years on *SCTV*."

One of the best things about appearing in *Splash* for John was how much money he made. He walked away with $350,000, the highest amount he had ever been paid for his work. The Disney Company, which made the film, guaranteed John $350,000 for any subsequent movies he would make with them.

John loved the idea of having financial power. However, he missed out on acting in another blockbuster film, a film much bigger than *Splash*. Canadian director Ivan Reitman asked John Candy to sign on with *Ghostbusters*. John had worked with Reitman in *Stripes*, and he had voiced a small part in a Reitman animated film called *Heavy Metal*. But John demanded Reitman pay him the same amount as Disney. Reitman refused, and John was left out of the wildly popular comedy. He would have been cast in the role that actor Rick Moranis ended up playing.

John later spoke about his decision: "Rick did a nice job with the part. Of course it would have been different with me, but I don't think it would have been right for me to lower my price for Ivan and then go back to Disney and collect a higher fee."

Reitman continued to make successful movies, but he never asked John to work for him again. And as for the deal John had made with Disney, subsequent shake-ups in the organization and some creative differences in opinion resulted in Candy never making another film for Disney.

Workaholic John decided to take a breather after making *Splash* to get his physical life in order. A popular diet regimen at that time was the Pritikin diet, invented by Nathan Pritikin. Pritikin himself had previously faced what could have been a deadly heart problem had he not decided to take matters into

     They Died Too Young

his own hands and drastically change his eating habits.

Pritikin ended up building a center to which people could come and learn to eat in a more healthy manner and exercise enough to successfully lose weight. John spent some time there and did end up losing 75 pounds. He had worried if he would have the same on-screen appeal if he were thinner. As he returned to making movies, it was apparent that Candy fans loved John Candy no matter what his size.

Photofest

***With Richard Pryor in the 1985 film* Brewster's Millions**

He teamed with comedian Richard Pryor in his next film, *Brewster's Millions.* John played the part of Pryor's friend in a plot which had Pryor's character spending a small fortune in order to gain a larger one. The movie ended up being a simple piece of fluff, for Pryor, at his best when he can act in an over-the-top manner, was tightly reined in by the script. John's performance was typical, likable Candy stuff, but even he could not boost the film to top box-office success.

The year 1985 was a particularly busy one for John Candy. He ended up signing for a record four films that year. People wondered if he would jump at any role, no matter how weak the script or skimpy the role. But John only felt fulfilled when he was working, so he tended to jump at practically anything that came his way.

Even the birth of his second child, a son he and Rose named Christopher and born toward the end of 1984, did not interfere with his personal work ethic.

After shooting *The Last Polka*, John looked to the projects ahead.

Filming the 1985 film Volunteers *in Mexico with costar Tom Hanks*

GOING NOWHERE FAST

Ahead was a stay in a remote part of Mexico called Tuxtepec for a couple months, where John Candy was once again teamed with his *Splash* costar Tom Hanks. They were brought together to make the movie *Volunteers*. The story, set in the 1960s, is about an obnoxious young rich kid (Hanks), who racks up an enormous gambling debt which he escapes by joining the Peace Corps.

The Peace Corps was the brainchild of President John F. Kennedy. Its purpose was to send college-educated American young people to ailing Third World countries in order to teach foreigners valuable life skills such as efficient methods of engineering or farming.

The film is supposed to be a spoof of the idealism which ran through the youth of America in the early '60s. John's character is that of an enthusiastic engineer. Hanks character alienates his compatriots in short order. John's engineer eventually is kidnapped and brainwashed to the point of spouting Communist slogans, and the whole movie gets bogged down with a decided lack of enthusiasm and without a sparkling script.

Once again, John was stuck in the mud with a dud of a film, hardly worth the months of separation from his family.

Even while he was in Mexico, John was making plans to appear in another movie, *Summer Rental*. Candy was not too crazy about the script when he read it in Tuxtepec, but he

On the set of Summer Rental *with* director Carl Reiner

was thrilled that he would be working with world-renowned comedian Carl Reiner, who was *Summer Rental*'s director.

He had no pangs of regret leaving the roach-infested confines of Tuxtepec to take the leading role in Carl Reiner's film. John played a beleaguered air-traffic controller in great need of a vacation who packs up his wife, his kids, and his car to embark on a beach vacation. Instead of getting a restful break from his high-stress job, the vacation turns into a comedic horror show.

Once again, John was leaving one project and immediately rushing into another whose very script indicated it, like many other movies he worked on, was not going to be an extraordinary film success. But John thought working with the famed Reiner would make it all worthwhile. The movie was made at breakneck speed.

"It was a *Guinness Book of World Records* movie," John later said of the production schedule. "We shot it in April and May and it came out in August. We didn't even have enough time to spend the whole budget."

John was excited about having the leading role and was paid $800,000 for his work, but it was harder work than playing a supporting character.

"I was in every scene," he later recalled. "I had to work every day, with no days off. There's a lot of pressure because you know they're spending eight million dollars on the pic-

They Died Too Young

ture. I ain't Rambo, I ain't Schwarzenegger. I thought, 'Geez, what if they don't make their money back?'"

Summer Rental was released in the summer of 1985 and actually did fairly well at the box office, thanks to Candy's ever-faithful fans. Another advantage of working with Carl Reiner was that, because John held the director in such high esteem, he took Reiner's kindly advice to return to his dieting and continue to try to lose weight for the good of his health. John had seldom allowed even his closest friends to express concern over his weight. Following *Summer Rental*, he did undertake some serious efforts to maintain a serious diet and exercise program.

Unfortunately, John followed this pleasant piece of film success with a disastrous effort called *Armed and Dangerous:* he was paired with his old friend Eugene Levy in this movie, which was directed by Mark Lester. John played a hapless policeman, and critics thought the entire movie should have been brought up on charges because they hated it so much. Film critic Paul Attanasio from the *Washington Post* made his feelings quite clear in his review of *Armed and Dangerous:* "It takes a director with true genius for disaster to put together John Candy and Eugene Levy, the fine character actors Kenneth McMillan and Robert Loggia, and the delicious new comic actress Meg Ryan and come up with a movie without a single laugh in it."

By this time, people were wondering just exactly what John Candy was doing with his career. Film critic Patrick Goldstein of the *Los Angeles Times* put the question in print in an article he wrote after the release of *Armed and Dangerous.*

"Eighteen months ago if you had asked people in Hollywood to pick a hot new comedy star, you could always have spotted John Candy's name near the top of the list. . . . What went wrong?"

John was sensitive to Goldstein's criticism and offered this defense of his film choices. "I'm always hearing about these great scripts. But then they say, 'Oh, it needs a rewrite.' Then before you know it, there's another rewrite, and then it needs a little polish, and by the time that has been done, the script is almost unrecognizable."

Between the summers of 1985 and 1986, John signed on for one scene in the comedic musical *Little Shop of Horrors* and did a short piece for a Canadian work called *The Canadian Conspiracy.*

By 1986, John had spent so much time in Hollywood that he decided it was time to move his family to the western film capital of the world. Good films or no, John had been able to command enough money for his screen work to buy a huge house in posh Brentwood, California, which had become home to many successful film and television stars, some of whom were also Canadians.

John wanted to be with his wife and young children as much as possible, so with the move completed, he was ready to take on his most successful project ever. But before that began, he had promised to work in a featured role with zany director Mel Brooks in perhaps John's most bizarre role. He was Barf, a half-man, half-dog creature in the movie *Spaceballs,* a silly Brooks attempt to spoof *Star Wars* and other science-fiction films. It did not come anywhere near Brooks's previous successes, but John was paid good money and had a lot of fun making *Spaceballs.*

As the lovable Barf in Mel Brooks's 1987 film, Spaceballs, *a satire of* Star Wars *and the modern science-fiction film genre*

Neal Page (Steve Martin) and Del Griffith (John Candy)
in the hilarious Thanksgiving 1987 movie release
Planes, Trains and Automobiles

BREAKTHROUGH AT LAST

The sun often shines on the hills and valleys of Hollywood, and fate certainly spilled some warm and fortunate rays onto John Candy's next film effort. *Planes, Trains and Automobiles* has come to be an all-time favorite film of John Candy and Steve Martin fans alike. The two actors were paired in this movie which director John Hughes brought to the screen in 1987.

Anyone who has ever attempted to get home for the holidays can identify with the nightmare trip Candy's and Martin's characters endured in the frigid Midwest as they tried to get to Chicago for Thanksgiving.

This was the movie John had been waiting for his whole career: a hilarious comedy which also moved viewers to tears of sympathy for the lonely bear of a man with the heart of gold.

The movie was released during Thanksgiving week in 1987, and moviegoers flocked to see it. *Planes, Trains and Automobiles* was not only a financial success. The critics, for the most part, also responded kindly to John's performance.

Washington Post film critic Hal Hinson was expansive in his praise of Candy: "This is Candy's bustout performance, the one where he puts it all together. Candy has never been more boisterously cracked."

John Candy had finally struck movie gold, and his association with John Hughes earned him a walk-on appearance in Hughes's 1988 film, *She's Having a Baby*. By the summer of that year, another Hughes film, *The Great Outdoors*, was released. It starred John Candy and old friend Dan Aykroyd in a farce about the rigors and horrors of extended family relationships. Unfortunately, the movie turned out to be a critical flop, as was Candy's next venture, a film shot in Canada called *Who's Harry Crumb?*

John was very optimistic that this movie about a bumbling detective would be well received because the producer, Arnon Milchan, had achieved success with several films in the past, such as *The King of Comedy* and *Brazil*. John was excited that, during production, Milchan allowed John a great deal of input as to how things should go. But in the end, it just did not come off as the laugh riot it was intended to be.

Although the runaway success of *Planes, Trains and Automobiles* had enabled him to command a whopping $3 million a picture, having that financial clout did not change John's pattern of jumping into whatever project presented itself, no matter how flimsy the script looked.

The ubiquitous John was actually in three movies which were released in 1989: *Who's Harry Crumb?*, *Speed Zone!*, and *Uncle Buck*. *Speed Zone!* was one of those *Cannonball Run* knockoffs, those cross-country, race-for-a-prize movies, none of which were noted for their inspired scripting. John did have a lot of fun participating in the movie's production despite its failure, and since he was paid a tidy sum for his efforts, he did not consider the experience a great loss. He was always sensitive to reviews and particularly upset by bad ones, and often he would abandon any attempt to diet when the press treated him negatively.

John Candy's friend Bernie Sahlins, from their Second City days, had some ideas about what happened with his friend John.

"When he hit it big in *Splash*, it was the right kind of role for John—reactive. Then with the usual Hollywood insanity they started throwing things at him that were wrong for him—leading man things. There are very few people who can keep a career perspective in the face of this kind of temptation. Rose was a great anchor and stabilizing influence, but finally you find yourself surrounded by advisers who tell you only what you want to hear. John enjoyed making a lot of money and feeling universally loved and being Johnny Toronto. And maybe he couldn't help himself. People in Hollywood live in some other world—rarified and remote. It's hard to say no. That's why Hollywood people keep failing upwardly."

Sahlins continued, "When you have power there's no one to thrust the truth on you because you're so powerful and most of the time you don't want to hear it. And if you're also famous, you can't go out to eat without fifty people looking to see whether you're using the right fork. In defense, you are forced to lead an artificial existence. At first, you are pleasantly surprised when you walk down the street and people mob you. Then after a while when they mob you, you're irritated. But if they ever stop mobbing you, then you get upset. You're caught in an absurd and deadly syndrome."

Another Candy associate, Martyn Burke, further pinpointed the dangers Candy faced as a part of the Hollywood scene.

"When you become successful in Hollywood," Burke said remembering his friend, "you have money, power and fame all being thrown at you. If you go after all of it at once, Hollywood will destroy you. John was too scattered and unfocused to make good choices. He got involved in a huge range of activities that would have been beyond anyone's capacity to handle. By the time he had to apply the brakes, it was too late. The wheels had come off."

As if he hadn't enough to do, John began producing and starring in a weekly two-hour radio show which began airing just as he went to Chicago to begin working on *Uncle Buck*.

With Macaulay Culkin in the 1989 film **Uncle Buck**

The radio show featured his beloved form of humor laced with comedic traffic reports. It showcased many of his old friends from his *SCTV* days.

John starred in *Uncle Buck* as the caretaker of his nieces and nephew. Fans of the star rate it as one of his most endearing roles in which he fumbles his way through the trials of dealing with his errant charges.

John had high hopes for this movie, which was yet another John Hughes film, but as it turned out, John's performance was the only highlight of the movie, although it was a commercial success.

In 1990 John had a bit part in another John Hughes offering, a Christmas release called *Home Alone* starring newcomer Macaulay Culkin. The public ate up the movie, and it ended up making an incredible $270 million. The only sad part was that John Hughes had offered John Candy a small part of the movie's profits for helping out in the movie. Ever the people-pleasing friend, John turned down the offer, which would have made him rich beyond his wildest dreams.

In 1991, John landed a starring role in the film *Delirious,*

They Died Too Young

in which he plays a writer of a soap opera, who, due to an accident, finds himself a character in his own script. On-screen, the writer is obviously lost in a ball of confusion, but not nearly so much as the paying audience who sat through this muddled affair. John gave his usual endearing performance, but as had happened throughout his career, he could not save the faulty film.

Finally in 1991, Dan Aykroyd and Candy reunited, but this time Aykroyd directed John in the starring role of *Nothing But Trouble.* The movie, which also

With screen legend Maureen O'Hara

featured Demi Moore and Chevy Chase, was so dismal, the movie trade paper *Box Office* advised moviegoers they should, "Eat poison before you are forced to sit through it."

John did enjoy a sweet starring role in another movie which was released in 1991—*Only the Lonely.* The movie dealt with a topic to which probably half of America could relate: overbearing parents of adult children. John costarred with veteran screen actress Maureen O'Hara, who played his domineering mother. John found making the film with O'Hara a pleasant experience, even though, once again, the loose script and casual

*As a southern lawyer confronting investigator Jim Garrison
(Kevin Costner) in Oliver Stone's 1991 film,* JFK

performances of the supporting actors left the movie floundering.

As if he was not doing enough between his frequent cameo appearances and not-so-frequent starring roles in the early 1990s, John, who had always been an avid football fan, became part owner of the Toronto Argonauts football team, together with hockey great Wayne Gretzky and Los Angeles Kings owner Bruce McNall. During the football season, he would often return to his hometown to watch his team perform.

John took on a small dramatic role in 1991 in the controversial Oliver Stone film *JFK,* a movie whose story line claimed the assassination of President John F. Kennedy in 1963 was a huge political conspiracy. John took his family with him to New Orleans for the filming of the scene he shared with Kevin Costner.

John played a southern lawyer who tries to hide from investigator Jim Garrison (Costner) what he really knows about the assassination. Critics agreed that John did just fine in this small but pivotal role.

In 1992, he worked again with friend Eugene Levy, who directed John in the lead role in *Once Upon a Crime.* Unfortunately, what didn't end up on the cutting room floor

They Died Too Young

was the sort of sorry film that Levy and Candy had made fun of during their *SCTV* days.

A most unique premise came to be the story line for what was to be John Candy's last film released before his untimely death. *Cool Runnings*, a charming bit of fluff about an Olympic bobsled team from the tropical land of Jamaica, caught the imagination and funny bone of the film-going public.

When John was promoting the film, he spoke of his role.

"From my character's point of view, these guys are a joke. They'll never succeed. We're in Jamaica. There are no sleds here, no snow. They have no idea what a bobsled is. Yet they're determined."

And the public bought it. The movie was a box-office hit.

Had John taken a much-needed break after the success of *Cool Runnings,* perhaps things might have turned out differently.

But as he was wont to do, he immediately took on another film which he frankly did not want to do, mainly because of where it was filmed. Candy had the starring role in a comedy filmed by documentary filmmaker Michael Moore in 1993 called *Canadian Bacon,* which ended up not being released until 1995. Then John promptly signed onto *Wagons East,* an attempt at comedy which was being shot on location in Durango, Mexico. The filming was to take several months. John joined the production in January 1994.

By this time, John was having trouble with his hips. He had been off his healthy eating and exercise regimen and had gained a good deal of weight, so he suffered breathing difficulties because of the high altitude of the Mexican site.

He did not like having to be away from his family. But ever the planner, he had already agreed to work again with producer/director Steven Spielberg on a movie based on the *Little Rascals.*

But that was down the road and far away from the discomfort of Mexico. While he was away, Candy also found out his football team was about to be sold without his knowledge. All in all, things were not going at all well for John.

And the worst of all came for those who knew and loved this big, funny, complicated bear of a man. Sometime after he retired for the night on March 4, 1994, John Franklin Candy died in his sleep of a heart attack at age 43.

A reporter for the *Toronto Sun* whom Candy had befriended years earlier remembered Candy's kind words to her as she struggled working as a maitre d', serving Candy, Gretzky, and McNall, new owners of the Argonauts at the time.

"I remember him chain-smoking, loving football, being a great father, but most of all, I remember the time he tried to persuade me to foresake journalism for acting. These are the things I remember about John Candy," said Trish Tervit. "You gotta do what you love," was his advice.

It was, without a doubt, advice that John Candy spent his whole life following.

Long-time friend, costar, and fellow-Canadian Eugene Levy was devastated at the news of his friend's death. "This country had lost its greatest export," he later said mournfully. Canadian movie producer/director Norman Jewison said as he remembered how he and John's friends would beg him to lose weight and quit smoking, "I think we've always been worried about John. But I don't think any of us were prepared for this."

John's old friend and business associate from his Second City days, Andrew Alexander, memorialized his friend: "The Second City was truly blessed to count John as one of its family members. The world was a funnier and more human place because of John."

At the end of *Planes, Trains and Automobiles,* Del Griffith confesses to Neal Page, "I don't have a home."

The beloved John Candy will always have a home in the hearts of movie fans and friends everywhere.

Filmography

1971 *Faceoff* (extra)
1973 *Class of '44* (bit part)
1975 *It Seemed Like a Good Idea at the Time*
1976 *Tunnelvision* (bit part)
Find the Lady
1978 *The Silent Partner*
Kavic the Wild Dog (bit part—made for TV)
1979 *Lost and Found* (bit part)
1941
1980 *The Blues Brothers*
Double Negative (cameo)
1981 *Heavy Metal* (voice only)
Stripes
1982 *It Came from Hollywood* (cohost of clips anthology)
1983 *Going Berserk*
National Lampoon's Vacation (cameo)
1984 *Splash*
1985 *Brewster's Millions*
Sesame Street Presents Follow That Bird (cameo)
The Last Polka
Summer Rental
Volunteers
1986 *Armed and Dangerous*

The Canadian Conspiracy
Little Shop of Horrors (cameo)
1987 *Spaceballs*
Planes, Trains and Automobiles
1988 *She's Having a Baby* (unbilled cameo)
The Great Outdoors
Hot to Trot (voice only)
1989 *Who's Harry Crumb?*
Speed Zone!
Uncle Buck
1990 *Home Alone* (extended cameo)
1991 *Delirious*
The Rescuers Down Under (voice only)
Nothing But Trouble
Career Opportunities (cameo)
Only the Lonely
JFK (cameo)
1992 *Boris and Natasha* (cameo)
Once Upon a Crime
1993 *Rookie of the Year* (cameo)
Cool Runnings
1994 *Hostage for a Day* (cameo for TV)
Wagons East
1995 *Canadian Bacon*

Chronology

1950 John Franklin Candy born October 31.
1955 John's father, Sidney, dies of heart attack at age 35.
1971 Performs in first professional play, *Creeps*.
1972 Joins Caravan theatre – a children's touring group.
1973 Joins Second City, Toronto; performs at Second City in Chicago.
1974 Appears on *Dr. Zonk and the Zunkins*.
1975 Performs at Second City site in Pasadena, California.

1976 Performs as a regular on *SCTV* for three years.
1979 Marries Rosemary Margaret Hobor in April.
1980 Jennifer Candy born.
1981 *SCTV* is resurrected and Candy performs on the show until it ends in 1983.
1984 Christopher Candy born.
1986 Moves family to California.
1987 Enacts most successful role in *Planes, Trains and Automobiles*.
1991 Becomes part owner of Toronto Argonauts football team.
1994 John Franklin Candy dies March 4 at the age of 43.

INDEX